Childhoods
of the
Presidents

Ronald Reagan

Childhoods *of the* Presidents

John Adams

George W. Bush

Bill Clinton

Ulysses S. Grant

Andrew Jackson

Thomas Jefferson

John F. Kennedy

Abraham Lincoln

James Madison

James Monroe

Ronald Reagan

Franklin D. Roosevelt

Theodore Roosevelt

Harry S. Truman

George Washington

Woodrow Wilson

Ronald Reagan

Tamra Orr

Mason Crest Publishers
Philadelphia

Produced by OTTN Publishing, Stockton, New Jersey

Mason Crest Publishers
370 Reed Road
Broomall, PA 19008
www.masoncrest.com

First printing

1 3 5 7 9 8 6 4 2

Library of Congress Cataloging-in-Publication Data

Orr, Tamra.
    Ronald Reagan / Tamra Orr.
        p.   cm.   (Childhood of the presidents)
    Summary: A biography of the fortieth president of the United
    States, focusing on his childhood and young adulthood.
    Includes bibliographical references and index.
        ISBN 1-59084-280-4
    1. Reagan, Ronald—Childhood and youth—Juvenile literature.
    2. Reagan, Ronald—Juvenile literature. 3. Presidents—United
    States—Biography—Juvenile literature. [1. Reagan, Ronald—
    Childhood and youth. 2. Presidents.] I. Title. II. Series.
    E877.2.O77 2003
    973.927'092—dc21   1-15-03
    [B]   J973.9   2002069226
                                      CHI $18.00
                                      UKR

Childhoods
of the
Presidents

Table of Contents

★★★★★★★★★★★★★★★★★★★★

★ *Introduction* ★

Alexis de Tocqueville began his great work *Democracy in America* with a discourse on childhood. If we are to understand the prejudices, the habits and the passions that will rule a man's life, Tocqueville said, we must watch the baby in his mother's arms; we must see the first images that the world casts upon the mirror of his mind; we must hear the first words that awaken his sleeping powers of thought. "The entire man," he wrote, "is, so to speak, to be seen in the cradle of the child."

That is why these books on the childhoods of the American presidents are so much to the point. And, as our history shows, a great variety of childhoods can lead to the White House. The record confirms the ancient adage that every American boy, no matter how unpromising his beginnings, can aspire to the presidency. Soon, one hopes, the adage will be extended to include every American girl.

All our presidents thus far have been white males who, within the limits of their gender, reflect the diversity of American life. They were born in nineteen of our states; eight of the last thirteen presidents were born west of the Mississippi. Of all our presidents, Abraham Lincoln had the least promising childhood, yet he became our greatest president. Oddly enough, presidents who are children of privilege sometimes feel an obligation to reform society in order to give children of poverty a better break. And, with Lincoln the great exception, presidents who are children of poverty sometimes feel that there is no need to reform a society that has enabled them to rise from privation to the summit.

Does schooling make a difference? Harry S. Truman, the only twentieth-century president never to attend college, is generally accounted a near-great president. Actually nine— more than one fifth—of our presidents never went to college at all, including such luminaries as George Washington, Andrew Jackson and Grover Cleveland. But, Truman aside, all the non-college men held the highest office before the twentieth century, and, given the increasing complexity of life, a college education will unquestionably be a necessity in the twenty-first century.

Every reader of this book, girls included, has a right to aspire to the presidency. As you survey the childhoods of those who made it, try to figure out the qualities that brought them to the White House. I would suggest that among those qualities are ambition, determination, discipline, education— and luck.

—ARTHUR M. SCHLESINGER, JR.

The Reagan family. From left: Jack, John Neil, Ronald, Nelle. The photo was taken around 1915, when Ronald was about four.

A Humble Start

Many American presidents have enjoyed privileged backgrounds. They have come from wealthy, respected, and *prominent* families. For example, the families of three of the first four presidents—George Washington, Thomas Jefferson, and James Madison—were among Virginia's landholding upper class. More recently, Franklin Delano Roosevelt, born into one of the oldest families in New York, spent an idyllic childhood on his parents' estate, at their vacation home, and in exclusive resorts in Europe. John F. Kennedy's father—one of the richest men in America—made a fortune in banking and finance and, later, served as ambassador to Great Britain; a grandfather on JFK's mother's side had been mayor of Boston. George Bush's father, too, was a wealthy banker who had served in the United States Senate. And of course, by the time George Bush's son, George W. Bush, entered politics, his family had become even more prominent.

In contrast with the privileged childhoods enjoyed by these men who went on to serve in the nation's highest public office, the man who became the 40th president of the United States came from a humble background. In some ways Ronald Reagan might be said to have grown up disadvantaged.

In a recent biography of President Reagan, *When Character Was King*, author Peggy Noonan (a former speechwriter for the president) writes, "Ronald Reagan's beginnings were the most modest and lacking of any president of the past hundred years." Reagan's family was never much respected in the community, because of his father's *alcoholism* and inability to hold a job. The Reagans never had a lot of money, never owned a farm or a successful business, and never even reached the middle class. As a young child, Ronald Reagan saw his family move so frequently that he hardly had the chance to call a place home before the bags were being packed again. His parents were from very different backgrounds— and this led to more than a few disagreements and problems.

Despite this difficult beginning, however, Ronald Reagan grew up to become one of this country's most beloved presidents. Nicknamed "the Great Communicator," he connected with the American people, many of whom felt he honestly understood them. He seemed to know where they were coming from, to understand the struggles they went through— because he had gone through many of the same struggles as a child.

In her book *When Character Was King*, Peggy Noonan relates a story that illustrates this. In 1987, when Ronald Reagan was president, a young staff member named Doug MacKinnon entered his office for a moment. The two began talking and suddenly MacKinnon blurted out, "Mr. President, my father had the same thing your father had." President

Ronald Reagan was born in his parents' small apartment on the second floor of this building in Tampico, Illinois, on February 6, 1911. At the time, a restaurant and bakery occupied the first floor.

Reagan knew right away that he was referring to alcoholism. In the next few minutes, the men shared the pain and the sadness that comes with watching a loved one battle the disease.

"He was really warm and he seemed to want to reach me," MacKinnon recalled. "He wanted to reach out and help someone who was going through what he had gone through. It was just a short visit but it told me everything I needed to know about Ronald Reagan—that he had an enormous heart, that he could empathize with people and that he wanted to make sure you knew he understood and felt for you. . . . That he could persevere and become what he became—to be the son or daughter of an alcoholic is a tough lifestyle to make it out of and many people don't, but he did."

A baby photo of Ronald, whom the family had nicknamed Dutch, with his older brother Neil, nicknamed Moon. As they grew, the brothers' vastly different personalities became evident.

Beginning in a Blizzard

The small town of Tampico, Illinois—population 1,276—was in the middle of a huge blizzard on February 6, 1911, and John "Jack" Reagan couldn't find Dr. Terry. Reagan was looking for the local physician because his wife, Nelle Wilson Reagan, was in labor with the couple's second child. In an era when automobiles were still a novelty and horses were the main mode of transportation, it took time for Jack Reagan to find help. Finally, he brought the area *midwife*, Mrs. Roy Rasine, to the couple's little apartment above the restaurant, where his wife waited.

Soon after the midwife's arrival, Ronald Wilson Reagan entered the world. When Jack saw the 10-pound newborn, he exclaimed, "He looks like a fat little Dutchman." That exclamation would lead to a lifelong nickname. To his friends and family, Ronald Reagan has always been known as "Dutch."

Jack and Nelle Reagan had been married for a little over six years when Ronald was born. They had first met over the store counter of the J. W. Broadhead Dry Good Store in Fulton, Illinois, where they both worked. They had wed in late 1904. Ronald's older brother, John Neil, had joined the family in late

1908 and was just over two when Dutch came along. Like his new sibling, John Neil had quickly gotten a nickname: "Moon," for a comic strip character of the time, Moon Mullins.

Moon and Dutch were quite different in personality and spent many of their growing years going in completely opposite directions. However, one time they banded together for a common goal. When Ronald was only a toddler, his brother led him to the Tampico railroad station and pointed out the ice wagon on the other side of the tracks. There was ice cream on that wagon and the boys were determined to get it. "[We] crawled under a train snorting steam in the station," Ronald Reagan recalled. "We got to the other side just before it gave a mighty jerk and chuffed out."

The boys' father, Jack Reagan, was a handsome, charming, first-generation Irish-American Catholic. Jack Reagan had lost his parents to *tuberculosis* when he was only six years old. He lived with various relatives until he turned 12 and left school to help out in his aunt and uncle's dry-goods store. Since he and Nelle had been married, he had struggled to hold a job, thanks to the terrible combination of bad luck and his heavy drinking. Despite his quick wit and ability to tell a wonderful story, Jack had trouble sticking with any job. He worked primarily as a shoe salesman in a variety of stores throughout Illinois. The constant shifting of jobs forced his family to move from town to town as he searched for work.

> "John Edward Reagan . . . was a man who might have made a brilliant career out of selling but he lived in a time—and with a weakness—that made him a frustrated man."
>
> —Ronald Reagan

Nelle Wilson came from a Scots-English family and grew up a devout Protestant. The youngest of six children, Nelle was a gentle, quiet woman who always saw the best in people. Even though she was keenly aware that Jack had a drinking problem, she taught her children and others to look on it as a sick-

> Moon and Dutch always called their parents by their first names, Nelle and Jack, rather than Mom and Dad. "Ours was a free family that loved each other up to the point where the independence of each member began," recalled Ronald Reagan. "For as long as I can remember, we were on a first-name basis with each other."

ness, rather than a character flaw. No matter how difficult life was in her own home as she fought to stretch money and keep food on the table, she still spent much of her time doing charity work and helping others. She would visit prisoners in jail and the sickest patients in the hospital.

"We were poor," Ronald Reagan said later in life, "[but] in those days, you didn't feel poor. . . . There was always someone worse off. My mother was always finding people to help." She was a strong believer in her faith and a very active member of the Disciples of Christ Church.

Nelle also had a flair for the dramatic. She loved acting and would sometimes take parts in local plays or do religious poetry readings for groups. Now and then, she would bring her two young sons along with her to perform. Surprisingly, it was John Neil who everyone thought would grow up to be a performer, as he was quite the talented singer and dancer.

Jack and Nelle loved each other, even though they were complete opposites in so many ways. As Ronald Reagan once put it, "If my father was Catholic, my mother was Protestant. If he rebelled against the universe, she was a natural practical do-gooder. . . . If he was occasionally *vulgar*, she tried to raise the tone of the family."

"No diploma was needed for kindness, in her opinion," he continued, "just as my father believed energy and hard work were the only ingredients needed for success."

In 1914, when Ronald was three years old, the family moved to the big city of Chicago. Jack had found a job as a shoe salesman in the Fair Store, and so everyone's belongings were packed and the little apartment was left behind. Unfortunately, the job lasted only a few months. Then, once again, the Reagans found themselves packing their bags and moving, this time to a town called Galesburg.

The family remained in Galesburg for a little over three years. The house they rented had an amazing collection of birds' eggs and butterflies stored in the attic. Young Ronald spent many hours up there, poring over these treasures and nurturing a newfound appreciation for the world of nature. "The colors and textures—and most especially the *fragility*— of these objects fascinated my imagination," he wrote. "They became gateways to the mysterious, symbols of the out of doors. . . . Here, in the musty attic dust, I got my first scent of wind on peaks, pine needles in the rains and visions of sunrise on the desert." He began taking long walks with his brother, and he studied the wildlife that he saw around him.

Nelle read aloud to both of her sons each evening. One night when Ronald was five years old, he picked up the news-paper and began looking through it. When Jack asked him

Ronald's third-grade class in Tampico, circa 1919. The future president (second row, left) appears deep in thought.

what he was doing, Ronald replied that he was reading. Both parents were astonished to find out that he truly was reading. He had learned by following along when his mother read to him. As Ronald Reagan later explained, "One evening all the funny black marks on paper clicked into place."

By 1918, changes were again coming to the Reagan household. Once more, Jack had lost his job. This time, he found a

Jack Reagan worked briefly at the Pitney General Store in Tampico (at right in this photo), but the Reagans were forced into another of their many moves after the store was sold.

position as a shoe clerk in the E. B. Colwell Department Store in nearby Monmouth, Illinois. During the family's time there, the town was hit by the *influenza* epidemic that was sweeping the country—and the entire world. In most years the flu isn't particularly dangerous to people who are otherwise healthy. But the strain that emerged in 1918 was different. It killed millions of people, and Nelle Reagan almost became one of those victims. Fortunately, after being sick for several weeks, Nelle began to recover.

The Reagans' stay in Monmouth was a brief one. By the following summer, the family had come full circle, moving back to Tampico. There Jack began working as the manager of the Pitney General Store.

As luck would have it, the owner, Mr. Pitney, decided to sell his store in 1920. He promised Jack part of the profit from the sale if Jack would stay until he shut the store down. But instead of following through on this promise, he gave Jack a percentage of another business he owned called the Fashion Boot Shop. This store was in Dixon, Illinois, a city of just over 8,000 people located about 25 miles from Tampico. On December 6, 1920, the Reagans packed up one more time and drove their first car, a used vehicle bought from Mr. Pitney, to Dixon. It was this city that Ronald Reagan would always refer to as his hometown. Here, finally, he was able to stay long enough to make friends and set down roots.

Ronald Reagan lived in this house after his family moved to Dixon, Illinois, in late 1920.

Dutch Reagan poses for a photo in Dixon, circa 1923. In later years he would look back fondly at his boyhood in the small Illinois city, which he always considered his hometown.

A Tom Sawyer Boyhood

*L*ife in Dixon was pleasant and simple. Later, Ronald Reagan would refer to it as a "Tom Sawyer boyhood," recalling the famous Mark Twain character. Located on the Rock River in Illinois, the city was about 100 miles from Chicago and was surrounded by rolling hills, farms, and countryside. Half the city's population worked in some kind of industry, such as the Reynolds Wire Company or the Clipper Lawn Mower Company.

Ronald's brother, John Neil, settled in quickly, as he usually did after the family's moves. Dutch took longer and was alone much of the time. As he had done in Galesburg, he spent time exploring and discovering the world outside his house. "That big gap of two years between Neil and myself was pretty apparent by this time," he wrote, "and we were each traveling our own paths."

The younger Reagan also passed the hours by drawing cartoons and reading. Among his favorite books were medieval tales of King Arthur and his noble Knights of the Round Table; adventure stories featuring Tarzan, the Rover Boys, and the Three Musketeers; detective stories about Sherlock Holmes and his partner, Dr. Watson; and the rags-to-riches tales of author Horatio Alger. Somehow, it escaped everyone's attention that young Ronald held his books only inches away from his face when reading.

His other passion was the movies. His favorite actor was Tom Mix, who starred in many of the silent Western movies made in the early 1900s. Ronald would save up a dime as often as he could, and he and his best buddy, Newt, would go to the local Saturday *matinee* and watch Tom Mix on the screen. Ronald also enjoyed listening to the radio. He liked to pretend that he was an announcer and would often use a broom handle for his microphone. He frequently entertained his family by making up stories and news reports and then acting them out with his "mike" in hand. No one could have guessed that years in the future, this wouldn't be an act: Ronald Reagan would work as a real radio announcer. And the practice he got pretending to be an announcer would come in handy when he had to describe baseball games he wasn't actually watching.

In the Reagan household, Jack was in charge of discipline, and he once gave Ronald a "licking" his son would never forget. Ronald and his friend Harold "Monkey" Winchell had been eager to look at a new gun Harold's father had bought. They sneaked over to the Winchells' and got it out to examine it. Moments later, a shot went through the ceiling. "There was a blast like

> "All of us have a place to go back to. Dixon is that place for me. There was the life that shaped my mind and body for all the years to come after."
> —Ronald Reagan

Ronald Reagan's passion for motion pictures began during childhood. As a boy, he particularly enjoyed Westerns starring the matinee idol Tom Mix.

WILLIAM FOX PRESENTS
Tom Mix
IN
THE BEST BAD MAN
from MAX BRAND'S great novel 'SENOR JINGLE BELLS'
WITH
· CLARA BOW · PAUL PANZER · CYRIL CHADWICK · JUDY KING ·
and *TONY*, the Wonder Horse
J.G. BLYSTONE PRODUCTION

doomsday," Ronald Reagan recalled. "We heard the thunder of feet on the stairs, the yells of alarm coming rapidly nearer." But other than terrifying the boys, the accidental gunshot did not do much damage—except to Ronald's rear end when Jack found out.

Another time Jack decided on a different type of punishment. As Ronald explained it later, "My father bought a carload of second hand potatoes. . . . My brother and I were ordered to . . . sort the good potatoes from the bad. . . . [We] sat in a stinking boxcar during hot summer . . . gingerly gripping *tubers* that dissolve[d] in the fingers with a dripping squish. . . . At last we got so queasy at the very look of spuds that we simply lied about the rest and dumped them all, good or bad. We got a near permanent dislike for potatoes in any form."

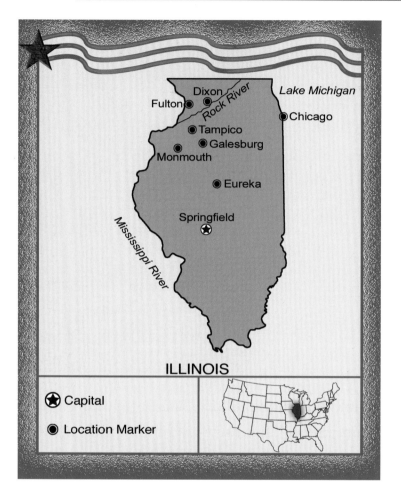

Dixon
Fulton
Rock River
Lake Michigan
Chicago
Tampico
Galesburg
Monmouth
Eureka
Springfield
Mississippi River

ILLINOIS

⭐ Capital

◉ Location Marker

During Ronald's childhood, the Reagans moved frequently throughout northern Illinois before settling in Dixon.

By the time Ronald was 11, he was aware that his father had a drinking problem. One day he came home from school to find Jack passed out on the front steps of their house. In his 1965 *autobiography*, *Where's the Rest of Me?*, he tells the story of when he realized that his dad was in trouble. "He was drunk, dead to the world. I stood over him for a minute or two. I wanted to let myself in the house and go to bed and pretend he wasn't there. . . . I bent over him, smelling the sharp odor of whiskey from the *speakeasy*. I got a fistful of his over-coat. Opening the door, I managed to drag him inside and get him to bed. In a few days he was the bluff, hearty man I knew and loved and will always remember." In a later autobiography, *An American Life*, written in 1990, Reagan added, "Sometimes he [Jack] went for a couple of years without a drop, but we never knew when he would suddenly decide to go off the wagon again and we knew that as soon as he touched one drink, the problem would start all over again."

More changes were ahead for Ronald. Now that his family was finally able to stay put for a while, it was time to learn more about who he was and what his future held.

Ronald didn't know it, but he was in for a wonderful surprise. He had enjoyed reading for years, and while he also enjoyed sports, he wasn't very good at them. "When I stood at the plate," he explained, "the ball appeared out of nowhere about two feet in front of me." One day, while on a drive with his parents and Moon, he found himself getting angry because they were reading signs along the road that he couldn't see. Finally, in frustration, he borrowed his mother's glasses and put them on his face. "Putting them on," he wrote, "I suddenly saw a glorious, sharply outlined world jump into focus and shouted with delight . . . the miracle of seeing was beyond believing. I was astounded to find out trees had sharply defined separate leaves; houses had a definite texture and hills really made a clear silhouette against the sky." No one had ever suspected he had a vision problem. Ronald hadn't realized it either; he thought everyone saw the world the way he did. Even his teachers hadn't caught on because he had such a good memory that he usually knew the right answers even if he couldn't begin to see the blackboard. His remarkable ability to memorize information would serve him well in a future that included film scripts and political speeches.

The miracle of sight came with an unexpected price, however. The glasses his mother got for him were large, black-rimmed things and Ronald hated them instantly. (He would get contact lenses in 1947, long before most people had even heard of them.) Despite his unhappiness with his new glasses, he had to admit that doing things like reading or going to the movies was a lot more fun now. So naturally, it wasn't long before he set his sights on doing well in sports.

Football, his favorite game since he had first played it in 1920 at age nine, was much easier now. In 1924 Ronald entered Dixon's Northside High School, a sturdy, redbrick building with a curriculum that focused on the arts and other cultural studies. Ronald wanted to be on the school's football team, but at only five feet three inches tall and just over 100 pounds, he was too small. It would take a summer or two of part-time jobs and hard work, as well as time to grow, for Ronald to fill out.

Meanwhile, despite his troubles with alcohol and the difficulty he had holding down a steady job, Jack Reagan managed to pass on some vital life lessons to his sons. He was passionately against any kind of *discrimination*, and he proved this to his family time and again. When Ronald was 10 years old, for example, D. W. Griffith's classic movie *Birth of a Nation* came to Dixon. Everyone in town was going to see it, and being a movie lover, Ronald really wanted to go. However, this was not even up for discussion in the Reagan household. Ronald

Reagan recalls his father telling him, "It deals with the Ku Klux Klan against the colored folks and I'm damned if anyone in this family will go see it."

A similar lesson came another time when Jack went to check into a small-town hotel. When the clerk assured him that he would like the hotel because it didn't allow any Jewish guests, Jack responded furiously. "I'm a Catholic," he said, "and if it's come to the point where you won't take Jews, you won't take me either." His devotion to fairness came with a price. Instead of staying at this hotel, he spent the cold winter night in his car, contracting *pneumonia* and, shortly after, experiencing his first heart attack.

Together with Nelle, Jack Reagan showed his boys the values of tolerance, fairness, generosity, faith, and discipline. These qualities would one day serve Ronald well in his role as leader of the country.

When D. W. Griffith's classic movie *Birth of a Nation* came to Dixon, Ronald desperately wanted to see it, but his father refused to let him because the film dealt with the racist Ku Klux Klan. Whatever his shortcomings, Jack Reagan always opposed prejudice of any kind.

4

During his teen years Ronald worked summers as a lifeguard. By his own count, he saved 77 people from drowning in the Rock River.

One Grand, Sweet Song

As he entered his teens, Ronald Reagan began working at a series of summer jobs. One of his first was for a construction contractor. He was paid 35 cents an hour for 10-hour days, six days a week.

At another job Ronald and his brother, Moon, worked together as *roustabouts* at the Ringling Brothers Circus. They dragged wagons around and fed the animals for 25 cents an hour. Ronald also had a part-time job as a *caddy* at a local golf course.

Without a doubt, however, his favorite job of all was as a lifeguard. Swimming was one skill he had mastered early; he didn't need to see well to swim. For seven years, Ronald was the lone lifeguard at Lowell Park, a 300-acre forested park next to the Rock River. He was paid $15 a week and all the hamburgers and sodas he wanted throughout the summer. He worked 12 hours a day, seven days a week.

On August 3, 1928, Ronald Reagan's picture was featured right on the front page of the *Dixon Daily Telegraph* for saving the life of a man who had been drowning in the Rock River. It wasn't his first or last rescue either. During his seven years as a lifeguard, he saved an incredible 77 people from drowning. He put notches on a nearby log to keep track of them.

"Not many thanked me," he recalled, "much less gave me a reward. . . . The only money I ever got was ten dollars for diving for an old man's upper plate [dentures] that he lost going down our slide.

"I got to recognize that people hate to be saved: almost every one of them later sought me out and angrily denounced me for dragging them to shore."

Besides providing him with spending money and allowing him to start saving for college, Ronald's summer jobs had the extra benefit of building up his muscles. At six feet tall and 165 pounds, he was no longer too small to play football. He won a starting position at right guard on the Northside High School team. He also played basketball and joined the track team.

As he succeeded at sports, Ronald discovered that he was now quite popular with the girls. He found a girlfriend, Margaret "Mugs" Cleaver, who introduced him to an activity that would play a huge part in the rest of his life: drama.

The head of Northside's drama club was a slim and quiet English teacher named B. J. Fraser. Ronald Reagan later recalled, "From him I learned almost all of what I know about acting today. . . . Fraser had the knack of quietly leading us into a performance, of making us think our roles instead of acting them out mechanically."

Fraser saw in young Ronald the talent it takes to truly sparkle on stage. Perhaps that was due, in part, to the dra-

> **"I loved three things: drama, politics and sports and I'm not sure they always came in that order."**
> —Ronald Reagan

"[It] is the last thing in our civilized life," Ronald Reagan would say of his favorite game, "where a man can physically throw himself, his full body, into combat with another man." He played football in high school and college.

matic flair that his mother, Nelle, had shown. As a high school junior, Ronald was cast as Ricky, the son in Philip Barry's *You and I*. The following year, he played the villain in George Bernard Shaw's *Captain Applejack*. "I learned that heroes are more fun," Reagan stated dryly.

Ronald graduated from high school in 1928. Next to his picture in the yearbook was written, "Life is just one grand, sweet song, so start the music." For him the music would start at nearby Eureka College, a Christian school. Afterward he embarked on a path that would lead him to fame and, eventually, to the highest elected office in the United States.

Official portrait of the 40th president, whose extraordinary ability to connect with the American people earned him the nickname "the Great Communicator."

"The Great Communicator"

Ronald Reagan is considered one of the most beloved presidents in the history of the United States. Often called "the Great Communicator," he had a genuine talent for knowing how to talk to the American people in ways they could appreciate and understand. Despite his success in politics, however, it was the silver screen and the glamour of Hollywood that started him on the road to fame.

Upon his graduation from Eureka College in 1932, Reagan began doing what graduates the world over do—he started looking for a job. During this time, however, jobs were scarce because the United States was in the midst of the Great Depression. Triggered by the stock market crash of 1929, the *depression* had caused many people to lose their jobs, their life savings, and even their homes and farms.

Although he dreamed of becoming an actor, Ronald Reagan knew his chances were slim, so he pursued a career in radio announcing instead. His first gig was as a sports announcer for WOC in Davenport, Iowa. He quickly advanced to being the sportscaster for WHO in Des Moines.

He covered Chicago Cubs and White Sox baseball games—without actually being at the ballparks himself. He made up his play-by-play description from information coming over the telegraph wires. Soon he had become well known locally.

In 1936, Reagan did his first *screen test*. Two days later, Warner Brothers Studios hired him. He moved to Hollywood, California, in the summer of 1937 and, at the age of 26, began making films. Over the next 27 years, Ronald Reagan would act in more than 50 movies.

In between movies, he found time to serve in the army during World War II (he narrated training films), marry and divorce actress Jane Wyman, marry actress Nancy Davis, and

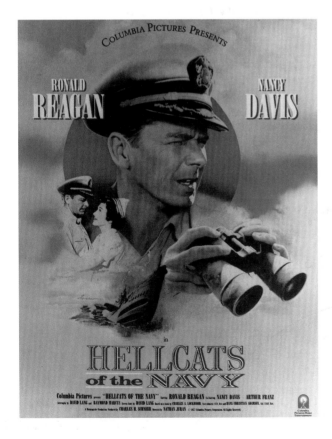

A publicity poster for *Hellcats of the Navy*, a 1957 film that starred Ronald Reagan and his wife, Nancy Davis Reagan.

become father to Maureen and Michael (with Wyman) and Patti and Ronald (with Nancy).

The turning point in his career, when he shifted from movie and television personality to politician, came in 1964. His longtime friend Barry Goldwater, a Republican senator from Arizona, was running for president, and Reagan agreed to help out by giving a televised fund-raising speech. Though Goldwater would lose the election, Reagan's speech inspired thousands of people to call in and contribute to the senator's campaign. Within a year, conservative Republicans were asking Ronald Reagan to run for governor of California.

His training in Hollywood helped Reagan win the race. He knew how to deliver a speech, how to time a punch line, when to look straight into the camera, and how to entertain large groups of people. Reagan served as California's governor from 1966 to 1974.

In 1976, he campaigned for the Republican Party's presidential nomination. He narrowly lost to Gerald Ford, the *incumbent* president. In the general election, Ford was defeated by Jimmy Carter.

In the 1980 presidential election, Reagan ran against Carter and won. At age 69, he became the oldest president ever elected. Four years later, he was reelected for a second term in a landslide victory over Walter Mondale.

Reagan's eight years in office were challenging and eventful. In 1981, he survived an *assassination* attempt by

> **"What I'd like to do is go down in history as the president that made Americans believe in themselves again."**
> **—Ronald Reagan**

A photographer snapped this picture in the first chaotic moments after John Hinckley's assassination attempt on Ronald Reagan, March 30, 1981. President Reagan, his press secretary James Brady, a Secret Service agent, and a policeman were all wounded in the shooting.

John W. Hinckley Jr., a 25-year-old man with a history of mental problems. The same year, Reagan fired all of America's air traffic controllers, who had gone on strike even though their contract prohibited them from doing so. Reagan's first year in office also produced a milestone for American women when the president nominated Sandra Day O'Connor to the Supreme Court. Confirmed by the Senate, O'Connor became the first woman to serve as a justice on the nation's highest court.

Overseas, Reagan claimed great achievements but also suffered significant setbacks. His most important foreign-policy success, without a doubt, came in his dealings with America's longtime Communist enemy, the Soviet Union. By greatly increasing U.S. defense spending, and by supporting groups that were fighting against the Soviets or their allies in regional conflicts all over the world, the president forced the Soviets to commit more of their resources to military spending. With its much smaller economy, the Soviet Union would be unable to keep pace with the United States in the long run.

Mikhail Gorbachev recognized this fact when he became the Soviet Union's leader in 1985. Gorbachev tried to ease tensions with the United States while restructuring the Soviet economy and reforming Soviet society. But limited new freedoms he permitted in the Soviet Union and the Eastern European countries it controlled raised people's expectations. One by one the Communist governments of Eastern Europe fell. And in 1991 the Soviet Union, too, collapsed. America had triumphed in its 45-year-long struggle with the Soviet Union—a struggle known as the Cold War—and many people believed that Ronald Reagan deserved much of the credit.

In other foreign-policy matters, things didn't turn out so well for the Reagan administration. The president committed U.S. marines to a

> "Not since Lincoln or Winston Churchill in Britain, has there been a president who has so understood the power of words to uplift and inspire."
> —Margaret Thatcher, former prime minister of Great Britain, describing Ronald Reagan

peacekeeping mission in the Middle Eastern country of Lebanon. But when terrorists drove a bomb-laden truck into the marines' barracks in Beirut, killing hundreds of American servicemen, the president withdrew the troops.

Perhaps the biggest failure of the Reagan years, though, was the so-called Iran-contra scandal. Although America's official policy was never to negotiate with terrorists, members of the Reagan administration sold arms to Iran in exchange for that hostile country's expected influence in obtaining the

The Reagan Presidential Library

Just northwest of Los Angeles, California, is a hill over-looking the Pacific Ocean. On that hill stands the Ronald Reagan Presidential Library and Museum. The dedication of the library and museum, in November 1991, was attended by President George H. W. Bush, the living former presidents (Richard Nixon, Gerald Ford, and Jimmy Carter), and, of course, Ronald Reagan.

The Spanish-style structure has four levels, two above ground and two below. The upper levels contain the museum, store, and foundation offices. The lower levels hold 55 million pages of government documents and papers, 1.5 million photographs, 769,000 feet of movie film, and more than 100,000 gifts given to the Reagan family.

The stated mission of the library is to promote the so-called Four Pillars of Freedom, which Reagan supported throughout his life: individual liberty, economic opportunity, global democracy, and national pride. More than 200,000 visitors come to the library each year to remember one of the most beloved presidents of all time, Ronald Reagan.

President Reagan shakes hands with Mikhail Gorbachev, general secretary of the Soviet Union's Communist Party, after the signing of a nuclear-missile treaty in 1988. Reagan administration policies are widely credited with hastening the collapse of communism in the Soviet Union and Eastern Europe, thus ending the Cold War.

release of American hostages being held by terrorists in Beirut. What's more, profits from the arms sales were channeled to the *contras*, revolutionaries trying to overthrow the

The Reagans dance at an inaugural ball kicking off the president's second term in office, January 21, 1985.

Communist government of Nicaragua. The U.S. Congress had earlier passed a law forbidding aid to the contras. When the illegal aid came to light, the Reagan administration suffered a major blow. But it was unclear what the president had known about the dealings, and he remained quite popular with the American people.

Although President Reagan had been diagnosed with colon cancer in 1985 and had undergone surgery, when he left the White House at the beginning of 1989 he seemed to be in good health. He and Nancy had many plans for an active retirement. Unfortunately, those plans were cut short in 1994 when Reagan was diagnosed with *Alzheimer's disease*, a health condition characterized by mental deterioration. Alzheimer's affects millions of older Americans every year.

In a courageous letter to the public announcing his condition, Reagan wrote, "I now begin the journey that will lead me into the sunset of my life. I know that for America there will always be a bright dawn ahead.

"Thank you, my friends. May God always bless you."

In an article in the November 14, 1994, issue of *Time* magazine, Hugh Sidey wrote, "He [Reagan] may not be able to win this battle [against Alzheimer's disease], but the way he's fighting it—with *candor* and courage—could be one of his most important legacies."

CHRONOLOGY

1911 Ronald Wilson Reagan is born in Tampico, Illinois.

1920 Family moves to Dixon, Illinois.

1924 Enters Northside High School.

1926 Gets job as a lifeguard at Lowell Park.

1927 Joins the high school drama club.

1928 Enrolls in Eureka College.

1932 Graduates from Eureka; becomes a sports announcer for WOC in Davenport, Iowa.

1937 Signs a contract with Warner Brothers; makes his first movie, *Love Is on the Air*.

1940 Marries actress Jane Wyman; plays one of his most famous roles, in the film *Knute Rockne—All American*.

1941 Daughter Maureen born; father, Jack Reagan, dies.

1942 Enters the army as a second lieutenant.

1945 Adopts son Michael.

1947 Elected president of the Screen Actors Guild.

1948 Divorces Jane Wyman.

1951 Marries Nancy Davis; daughter Patti born.

1958 Son Ronald Prescott Reagan born.

1962 Mother, Nelle Wilson Reagan, dies.

1964 Makes last film, *The Killers*.

1966 Elected governor of California.

1970 Wins second term as governor.

1980 Defeats incumbent, Jimmy Carter, to become the 40th president of the United States.

1981 Survives an assassination attempt; nominates Sandra Day O'Connor as first woman on the U.S. Supreme Court.

1984 Wins second presidential term in a landslide victory over Walter Mondale.

1985 Diagnosed with colon cancer; tumor is removed.

1986 Iran-contra scandal revealed.

1994 Diagnosed with Alzheimer's disease.

alcoholism—a disease in which a person cannot control his or her compulsion to drink alcoholic beverages.

Alzheimer's disease—a condition affecting the brain whose symptoms include memory loss, confusion, and personality changes.

assassination—the murder of a political or public figure.

autobiography—a book written about a person's life by that same person.

caddy—a person hired to carry a golfer's clubs.

candor—honesty, sincerity, or openness in expression.

depression—a period of very low economic activity, usually accompanied by high levels of unemployment.

discrimination—unfair treatment of people based on their religion, race, sex, or age.

fragility—the quality of being fragile or easily broken.

incumbent—the current holder of a political office.

influenza—a disease, caused by a virus, whose symptoms include fever, severe aches and pains, and infection of the respiratory tract; also called the flu.

matinee—a daytime showing of a movie or performance of a play.

midwife—a woman who helps in the delivery of babies.

pneumonia—a disease in which the lungs become inflamed, making it difficult to breathe.

prominent—widely known or distinguished.

roustabout—a circus worker.

screen test—a brief movie sequence filmed to test the ability of a new actor or actress.

speakeasy—a place where people can illegally get and drink alcohol.

tuberculosis—a disease of the lungs that is caused by bacteria and can easily be passed from one person to another.

tuber—a fleshy, usually underground stem of a plant, such as the potato, bearing buds from which new plant shoots arise.

vulgar—marked by a lack of good manners; rude or disgusting.

FURTHER READING

Devaney, John. *Ronald Reagan: President*. New York: Walker and Company, 1990.

Feinstein, Stephen. *The 1980s: From Ronald Reagan to M-TV*. Springfield, N.J.: Enslow Publishers, 2000.

Gallick, Sarah. *Ronald Reagan: The Pictorial Biography*. New York: Michael Friedman Publishing Group, Inc., 1999.

Johnson, Darv. *The Reagan Years*. San Diego: Lucent Books, 2000.

Joseph, Paul. *Ronald Reagan*. Edina, Minn.: Checkerboard Library, 1999.

Judson, Karen. *Ronald Reagan*. Springfield, N.J.: Enslow Publishers, 1997.

Kent, Zachary. *Ronald Reagan*. Chicago: Childrens Press, 1989.

Klingel, Cynthia Fitterer, and Robert B. Noyed. *Ronald W. Reagan: Our Fortieth President.* Chanhassen, Minn.: Child's World, 2001.

Larsen, Rebecca. *Ronald Reagan*. Danbury, Conn.: Franklin Watts, 1994.

Reagan, Ronald. *Where's the Rest of Me? The Autobiography of Ronald Reagan*. New York: Karz Publishers, 1965.

Spada, James. *Ronald Reagan: His Life in Pictures*. New York: St. Martin's Press, 2000.

Sullivan, George. *Ronald Reagan*. New York: Julian Messner, 1985.

- http://www.reaganlibrary.net
  The Ronald Wilson Reagan Presidential Library and Museum

- http://www.reagan.com
  The Reagan Information Interchange from son Michael Reagan

- http://www.reagan.utexas.edu
  Official website of the Ronald Reagan Presidential Library

- http://www.reaganlegacy.org
  Ronald Reagan Legacy Project

- http://www.reaganfoundation.org
  Ronald Reagan official presidential website

- http://www.reagan.navy.mil/
  US Navy website featuring the USS *Ronald Reagan* warship

INDEX

PICTURE CREDITS

Contributors

ARTHUR M. SCHLESINGER JR. holds the Albert Schweitzer Chair in the Humanities at the Graduate Center of the City University of New York. He is the author of more than a dozen books, including *The Age of Jackson*; *The Vital Center*; *The Age of Roosevelt* (3 vols.); *A Thousand Days: John F. Kennedy in the White House*; *Robert Kennedy and His Times*; *The Cycles of American History*; and *The Imperial Presidency*. Professor Schlesinger served as Special Assistant to President Kennedy (1961–63). His numerous awards include the Pulitzer Prize for History; the Pulitzer Prize for Biography; two National Book Awards; the Bancroft Prize; and the American Academy of Arts and Letters Gold Medal for History.

TAMRA ORR is a freelance writer living in Portland, Oregon. She writes on many different topics of interest to children and families. Her books include *The Korean Americans, Native American Medicine, Turkey, School Violence,* and *The Parent's Guide to Homeschooling*. She also writes for many national magazines and testing companies. She is very happily married and mom to four children who, she says, teach her more every day.